Animal Peculiarity Part 8

By T.P Just

~~~

Copyright © 2010 by Terence Just. All rights reserved.

I0436061

Get All The Books In The Series:

Table of Contents

1 Prologue

THERE is perhaps nothing extraordinary in the fact that man is wise and just, takes great care to provide for his own children, -shows due consideration for his parents, seeks sustenance for himself, protects himself against plots, and possesses all the other gifts of nature which are his. For man has been endowed with speech, of all things the most precious, and has been granted reason, which is of the greatest help and use.

Moreover, he knows how to reverence and worship the gods. But that dumb animals should by nature possess some good quality and should have many of man's amazing excellences assigned to them along with man, is indeed a remarkable fact. And to know accurately the special characteristics of each, and how living creatures also have been a source of interest no less than man, demands a trained intelligence and much learning. Now I am well aware of the labour that others have expended on this subject, yet I have collected all the materials that I could; I have clothed them in untechnical language, and am persuaded that my achievement is a treasure far from negligible. So if anyone considers them profitable, let him make use of them; anyone who does not consider them so may give them to his father to keep and attend to.

For not all things give pleasure to all men, nor do all men consider all subjects worthy of study. Although I was born later than many accomplished writers of an earlier day, the accident of date ought not to mulct me of praise, if I too produce a learned work whose ampler research and whose choice of language make it deserving of serious attention.

Mythology, mariners' yarns, vulgar superstitions, the ascertained facts of nature—all serve to adorn a tale and, on occasion, to point a moral. His religion is the popular stoicism of the age. Aleian repeatedly affirms his belief in the gods and in divine providence; the wisdom and beneficence of Nature are held up to veneration; the folly and selfishness of man are contrasted with the untaught virtues of the animal world. Some animals, to be sure, have their failings, but he chooses rather to dwell upon their good qualities, devotion, courage, self-sacrifice, gratitude. Again, animals are guided by reason, and from them we may learn contentment, control of the passions, and calm in the face of death.

2The 'Inflater' Fish

Leonidas of Byzantium asserts that there occurs in the Red Sea a fish of exactly the same size as a full-grown goby: it has neither eyes nor mouth after the manner of fishes, but grows gills and a kind of head, so far as one can guess, though its form is not perfectly developed.

But lower down beneath its stomach is a slightly indented depression which emits the colour of an emerald; and this, they say, is both its eye and its mouth. But anyone who eats it has fished to his own undoing.

And this is how he is destroyed: the man who has eaten it swells up; then his stomach bursts and he dies. But the fish itself when caught pays for it, for first, when it is out of the water, it swells, and if one touches it, it swells even more; while if one continues to handle it, it turns to corruption and becomes quite trans- lucent, like a man with dropsy, and finally bursts.

If however one is prepared to return it still a-live to the sea, it swims on the surface like an inflated bladder. Leonidas says that in consequence of this property man call it the 'inflater .'

3 The Seal

The Seal, I am told, vomits up the curdled milk from its stomach so that epileptics may not be cured thereby. Upon my word the Seal is indeed a malignant creature.

4 The Pelican

Pelicans that live in rivers take in mussels and then swallow them, and when they have warmed them deep within the recesses of their belly, they disgorge them.

Now the mussels open under the influence of the heat, just like the shells of things when cooked, and the Pelicans scoop out the flesh and make a meal.

5 The Sea-mew

So too Sea-mews, as Eudemus observes, lift snails into the air and carry them high up and then dash them violently upon the rocks.

6 Bear and two Lions

Eudemus records how on mount Pangaeus in Thrace a Bear
came upon a Lion's lair which was unguarded and slew the
Lion's cubs, they being small and unable to protect
themselves. But when the father and mother returned from
hunting somewhere and saw their young ones slaughtered,
they were naturally filled with grief, and set upon the Bear.
She in terror ran up a tree as fast as her legs could carry her
and sat there trying to escape their fell de- sign. But as they
came there with the intention of wreaking vengeance upon the
murderer, the Lioness did not relax her watch but sat down
beneath the tree-trunk, lying in Wait and gazing upward with
a look that meant blood.

Meantime the Lion in anguish and distraught with grief
roamed the mountains and came upon a woodcutter. The man
was terrified and dropped his axe, but the animal fawned
upon him and reaching upwards greeted him as well as it
could, stroking his face with its tongue.

And the man took courage, while the Lion, wrapping its tail around him, led him on and would not permit him to leave the axe but signified with its paw that he was to pick it up. But since the man failed to under- stand, the Lion took it in its mouth and offered it to him; the man followed and the Lion led him to the lair.

As soon as the Lioness saw him she too came up and began to fawn upon him with a piteous expression as she looked up at the Bear. So the man grasped their meaning and guessing that they had been somehow injured by the Bear, began to fell the tree with all the strength of his hands.

And the tree was overturned and the Bear brought down and the Lions tore her to pieces. As for the man, the Lion brought him back untouched and unscathed to the spot Where it first met him and restored him to his original task of cutting wood.

7 Ichneumon and Asp

A battle between two animals of Egypt, the Asp and the
Ichneumon. . . . The Ichneumon does not attack his adversary
without deliberation or rashly, but like a man fortifying
himself with all his weapons, rolls in the mud and covers
himself with a hard coating, thereby obtaining, it seems, an
adequate and impenetrable defence.
But if he is at a loss for mud, he washes himself in water and
plunges still wet into deep sand — a device which secures his
protection in difficult circumstances — and goes forth to battle.
But the tip of his nose, which is sensitive and somewhat
exposed to the bite of the Asp, he protects by bending back his
tail, thereby blocking the approach to it.
If however the Asp can reach it, the snake kills its adversary;
otherwise it plies its fangs against the mud in vain, while the
Ichneumon on the other hand makes a sudden dash, seizes the
Asp by the neck, and strangles it.
And the victory goes to the one that gets in first.

8 The Stork

When their parents have grown old, Storks tend them voluntarily and with studied care: yet there is no law of man that bids them do so; the cause of their actions is Nature. And the same birds love their offspring too.

Here is the proof: when the full grown bird is in want of food to give to its still unfledged and tender chicks, some accident having occasioned a shortage, the Stork disgorges its food of yesterday and feeds its young. And I am told that Herons do the same and Pelicans also.

Its migrations

I learn further that Storks migrate along with Cranes and all together avoid the winter. But when the season of frost is over and both Storks and Cranes return to their own homes, each kind recognises its own nests, as men do their own houses.

Transformed into a human being

Alexander of Myndus asserts that when they reach old age they pass to the islands of Ocean and are transformed into human shape, and that this is a reward for their filial piety towards their parents, since, if I am not mistaken, the gods especially desire to hold up there if nowhere else a human model of piety and uprightness, for in no other country under the sun could such a race continue to exist.

This is in my opinion no fairy-tale, otherwise what was Alexander's design in relating such marvels when he had nothing to gain from it? Anyhow it would have ill become an intelligent man to sacrifice truth to falsehood, be the gain never so great, still less if he was going to fall into an opponent's grasp, from which act nothing whatsoever was to be gained.

9. The Swallow and its nest

Whenever there is plenty of mud the Swallow brings it in her claws and builds her nest. If however mud is lacking, as Aristotle says, she souses herself in water and plunging into dust befouls her feathers.

Then when the mud has stuck to her all over, she scrapes it off by degrees with her beak and constructs her proposed dwelling. And as her young are tender and unfledged, she knows full well that if she lets them rest on bare twigs, they will suffer and be in pain.

Accordingly she settles on the backs of sheep, plucks some wool, and with it makes their bed soft for her offspring.

The Swallow and its young

The mother Swallow trains her young ones to be just by carefully distributing food in equal portions.

So she does not bring one meal for all, because she is not able
to do so, but brings small objects and a few at a time; she feeds
the first-born first, after it the second, thirdly her third
offspring, proceeding as far as the fifth in the same way; for
the Swallow neither conceives nor hatches more than five.
She herself only consumes as much food as she can obtain in
the nest, that is, anything that is dropped beside it. Her young
are slow to open their eyes, in the same way as puppies.
But she collects and brings a herb, and they by degrees gain
their sight; then after remaining quiet for a while, when able
to fly, they leave the nest to seek for food. Men long to possess
this herb but have not yet obtained their desire.

10 The Hoope

Among birds Hoopoes are the most savage; and in my opinion it is due to the recollection of their former existence as human beings and more especially from their hatred of the female sex, that they build their nests in desolate regions and on high rocks.

And to prevent human beings from getting near their young they smear their nests not with mud but with human excrement, and by dint of its disgusting and evil smell they repel and keep away the creature that is their enemy.

It happened that this bird had raised a family in the deserted part of a fortress, in the cleft of a stone that had split with age. So the guardian of the fortress, observing the young birds inside, smeared the hole over with mud.

When the Hoopoe returned and saw itself excluded, it fetched a herb and applied it to the mud. The mud was dissolved; the bird reached its young, and then flew off to get food. So once again the man smeared the spot over, and the bird by means of the same herb opened the hole.

And the same thing happened a third time. Therefore the guardian of the fortress, seeing what was done, himself gathered the herb

11 The Peloponnese devoid of Lions

The Peloponnese does not breed Lions, and Homer (as you would expect) with his trained intelligence realising the fact, says in singing of Artemis and her hunting there that she passes over Taygetus and Erymanthus And since these mountains are destitute of Lions he was quite right not to mention this.

12 The Perseus fish

There occurs in the Red Sea a fish, and, so far as I know, the people there have given it the name of Perseus. And the Greeks call it so, and the Arabians in like manner with the Greeks. For they too call Perseus the son of Zeus, and it is after him that they declare the fish is named.

Its size is that of the largest anthias; in appearance it is like a basse; its nose is somewhat hooked, and it is dappled with rings as it were of gold round its body, and these rings be- gin at the head at right angles to it and cease at the belly, It is armed with large teeth set close.

It is said to surpass other fish in-the strength and power of its body, neither is it wanting in courage. How to fish for it and how to catch it I have explained elsewhere.

13 Pinna and crab

The Pinna is a marine creature and belongs to the class of bivalves. It opens by parting the shells that enclose it, and extends a small piece of its flesh like a bait to fish that swim by.

The Crab however remains by its side, sharing its food and it's feeding- ground. So when some fish comes swimming up, the Crab gives the Pinna a gentle prick, where at the Pinna opens its shell wider and admits the head of the approaching fish - for it lowers its head to feed-and eats it.

14 The Cuckoo

Should be acquainted with these facts as well. The Cuckoo is extremely clever and most adroit at devising ingenious solutions to difficulties. For the bird is conscious that it cannot brood and hatch eggs because of the cold nature of its bodily constitution, so they say.

Therefore, when it lays its eggs, it neither builds itself a nest nor nurses its young, but watches until birds that have nestlings are flown and abroad, enters the strange lodging, and there lays its eggs.

The rascal does not however assail the nests of all birds, only those of the lark, the ring-dove, the greenfinch, and the pappus, knowing as it does that these birds lay eggs resembling its own. And if the nests are empty, it will not go near them, but if they contain eggs, then it mixes its own with them.

But if the eggs of the other bird are numerous, it rolls them out and destroys them and leaves its own behind, their resemblance making it impossible to know them apart and detect them. And the aforesaid birds hatch the eggs which are none of theirs.

But when the Cuckoo's young have grown strong and are conscious of their bastardy, they fly away and resort to their parent. For directly they are fledged they are recognised as alien and are grievously ill-treated.

The Cuckoo is seen only at one season, and that the best, of the year. For it is actually visible from the beginning of spring until the rising of the Dog-star; after that it withdraws from the sight of man.

15 The Cock, feared by Lion and Basillisk

The Lion dreads a Cock, and the Basilisk, they say, goes in fear of the same bird: at the sight of one it shudders, and at the sound of its crowing it is seized with convulsions and dies. This is why travelers in Libya, which is the nurse of such monsters, in fear of the aforesaid Basilisk take with them a Cock as companion and partner of their journey to protect themselves from so terrible an infliction.

16 Local Peculiarities

Crete is exceedingly hostile to wolves and rep- tiles; and I learn from Theophrastus that there are places on Macedonian Olympus where wolves do not go.

Goats in Cephallenia go without drinking for six months. Among the Budini, they say, you will not see a white sheep: they are all black.

It seems that one peculiarity that distinguishes animals consists in this: some bite and inject poison from a fang; while others are given to striking and having struck also inject a like deadly substance.

17 In Egypt

There are Goats in Egypt that produce quintuplets, while most produce twins. The Nile is said to be the cause of this, as the water it provides is extremely progenitive.
For that reason shepherds who like fine flocks and devote much care to them have a device for drawing as much water as is possible from the Nile for their herds, especially for animals that are barren.

Goats in Scyros

It is said that the Cows of Epirus give a most copious supply of milk, and the Goats of Scyros a far more generous yield than any other goats.

The Asp in Libya

The Libyan Asp, I am told, blinds the sight of the man who faces its breath. But the other kind does not indeed blind but kills at once.

A wonderful Horn

They say that a horn was brought from the Indies to Ptolemy II, and it held three amphorae. Imagine an ox that could produce a horn of that size.

Get All The Books In The Series:

Animal Peculiarity Part 1
Animal Peculiarity Part 2
Animal Peculiarity Part 3
Animal Peculiarity Part 4
Animal Peculiarity Part 5
Animal Peculiarity Part 6
Animal Peculiarity Part 7
Animal Peculiarity Part 8

www.ingramcontent.com/pod-product-compliance
Lightning Source LLC
Chambersburg PA
CBHW050922290526
45792CB00002B/855